MW00929434

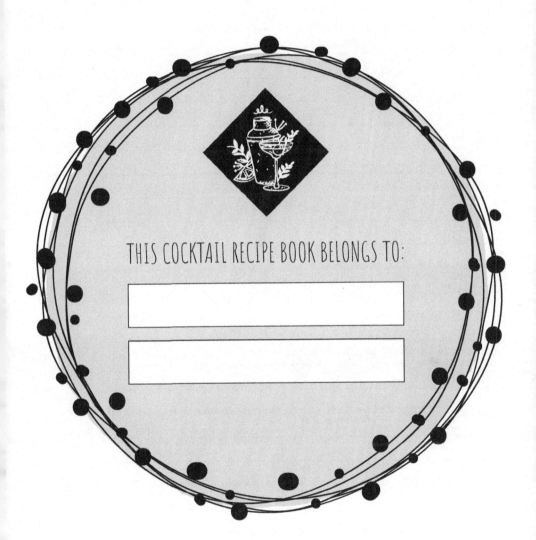

THIS COCKTAIL RECIPE BOOK BELONGS TO:

MY AWESOME COCKTAIL RECIPES

RECIPE

PAGE

MY AWESOME COCKTAIL RECIPES

RECIPE

PAGE

MY AWESOME COCKTAIL RECIPES

RECIPE

PAGE

MY AWESOME COCKTAIL RECIPES

RECIPE

PAGE

MEASUREMENT CONVERSION CHART

CUPS, SPOONS & LIQUIDS

MEASURE	OUNCES	EQUIVALENTS	LITERS
1/4 tsp			1 ml
1/2 tsp			2.5 ml
1 tsp		1/3 Tbsp	5 ml
2 tsp	1/3 fl oz	2/3 Tbsp	10 ml
1 Tbsp	1/2 fl oz	3 tsp	15 ml
2 Tbsp	1 fl oz	1/8 cup (6 tsp)	30 ml
1/4 cup	2 fl oz	4 Tbsp	60 ml
1/3 cup	2 2/3 fl oz	5 Tbsp & 1 tsp	80 ml
1/2 cup	4 fl oz	8 Tbsp	120 ml
2/3 cup	5 1/3 fl oz	10 Tbsp & 2 tsp	160 ml
3/4 cup	6 fl oz	12 Tbsp	180 ml
7/8 cup	7 fl oz	14 Tbsp	200 ml
1 cup (1/2 pint)	8 fl oz	16 Tbsp	220 ml
2 cups (1 pint)	16 fl oz	32 Tbsp	250 ml
1 quart	32 fl oz	4 cups	950 ml
1 quart plus 1/4 cup	34 fl oz	4 cups & 4 Tbsp	1 L
1 gallon (4 quarts)	128 fl oz	16 cups	3.8 L

WEIGHT

OUNCES	POUNDS	GRAMS
1/4 ounce		7 g
1/2 ounce		15 g
3/4 ounce		21 g
1 ounce		28 g
2 ounces		57 g
3 ounces		85 g
4 ounces	1/4 pound	113 g
8 ounces	1/2 pound	227 g
16 ounces	1 pound	454 g
35.2 ounces	2.2 pounds	1 kg

TEMPERATURE

FAHRENHEIT	CELSIUS
250° F	120° C
275° F	140° C
300° F	150° C
325° F	160° C
350° F	180° C
375° F	190° C
400° F	200° C
425° F	220° C
450° F	230° C
475° F	245° C

COCKTAIL

01 DATE .... DIFFICULTY ○ ○ ○ ○ ○ RATING ☆ ☆ ☆ ☆ ☆

INGREDIENTS

DIRECTIONS

GLASS

GARNISH

NOTES

COCKTAIL ....

01 DATE .... DIFFICULTY ○ ○ ○ ○ ○ RATING ☆ ☆ ☆ ☆ ☆

INGREDIENTS

....
....
....
....
....
....
....
....
....
....
....

DIRECTIONS

....
....
....
....
....
....
....
....
....
....
....
....

GLASS

GARNISH ....
....
....
....

NOTES ....
....
....
....
....

COCKTAIL ....

📅 DATE ....   DIFFICULTY ○○○○○   RATING ☆☆☆☆☆

🍾 INGREDIENTS

🍸 DIRECTIONS

🥂 GLASS

🌿 GARNISH ....

📝 NOTES ....

COCKTAIL ....

📅 **01** DATE .... DIFFICULTY ○ ○ ○ ○ ○ RATING ☆ ☆ ☆ ☆ ☆

INGREDIENTS

DIRECTIONS

🍷 GLASS

🍹 GARNISH ....

📝 NOTES ....

COCKTAIL _____

📅 **01** DATE _____   DIFFICULTY ○○○○○   RATING ☆☆☆☆☆

🍾 **INGREDIENTS**

🍸 **DIRECTIONS**

🍷 **GLASS**

🌿 **GARNISH** _____

📝 **NOTES** _____

COCKTAIL

DATE _____ **DIFFICULTY** ○ ○ ○ ○ ○ **RATING** ☆ ☆ ☆ ☆ ☆

INGREDIENTS

DIRECTIONS

GLASS

GARNISH

NOTES

COCKTAIL

DATE .... DIFFICULTY ○ ○ ○ ○ ○ RATING ☆ ☆ ☆ ☆ ☆

INGREDIENTS

DIRECTIONS

GLASS

GARNISH

NOTES

COCKTAIL

DATE ....

DIFFICULTY ○ ○ ○ ○ ○

RATING ☆ ☆ ☆ ☆ ☆

INGREDIENTS

DIRECTIONS

GLASS

GARNISH

NOTES

COCKTAIL ....

01 DATE .... DIFFICULTY ○○○○○ RATING ☆☆☆☆☆

INGREDIENTS

DIRECTIONS

GLASS

GARNISH ....

NOTES ....

COCKTAIL

DATE _____ **DIFFICULTY** ○ ○ ○ ○ ○ **RATING** ☆ ☆ ☆ ☆ ☆

INGREDIENTS

DIRECTIONS

GLASS

GARNISH

NOTES

COCKTAIL

INGREDIENTS

DIRECTIONS

GLASS

GARNISH

NOTES

COCKTAIL

01 DATE _____ DIFFICULTY ○ ○ ○ ○ ○ RATING ☆ ☆ ☆ ☆ ☆

INGREDIENTS

DIRECTIONS

GLASS

GARNISH

NOTES

COCKTAIL

DATE _____ DIFFICULTY ○○○○○ RATING ☆☆☆☆☆

INGREDIENTS

DIRECTIONS

GLASS

GARNISH

NOTES

19

COCKTAIL

DATE _____ **DIFFICULTY** ○ ○ ○ ○ ○ **RATING** ☆ ☆ ☆ ☆ ☆

INGREDIENTS

DIRECTIONS

GLASS

GARNISH

NOTES

COCKTAIL ....

📅 DATE ....   DIFFICULTY ○○○○○   RATING ☆☆☆☆☆

🍾 INGREDIENTS

🍸 DIRECTIONS

🍷 GLASS

🌿 GARNISH ....
....
....

📝 NOTES ....
....
....
....

COCKTAIL

DATE _____ **DIFFICULTY** ○ ○ ○ ○ ○ **RATING** ☆ ☆ ☆ ☆ ☆

INGREDIENTS

DIRECTIONS

GLASS

GARNISH

NOTES

COCKTAIL

DATE .... DIFFICULTY ○○○○○ RATING ☆☆☆☆☆

INGREDIENTS

DIRECTIONS

GLASS

GARNISH

NOTES

COCKTAIL

01 DATE .... DIFFICULTY ○ ○ ○ ○ ○ RATING ☆ ☆ ☆ ☆ ☆

INGREDIENTS

DIRECTIONS

GLASS

GARNISH ....

NOTES ....

COCKTAIL

DATE .... **DIFFICULTY** ○ ○ ○ ○ ○ **RATING** ☆ ☆ ☆ ☆ ☆

INGREDIENTS

DIRECTIONS

GLASS

GARNISH

NOTES

COCKTAIL

DATE _____ DIFFICULTY ○○○○○ RATING ☆☆☆☆☆

INGREDIENTS

DIRECTIONS

GLASS

GARNISH

NOTES

COCKTAIL

DATE _____   DIFFICULTY ○○○○○   RATING ☆☆☆☆☆

INGREDIENTS

DIRECTIONS

GLASS

GARNISH

NOTES

COCKTAIL

01 DATE _____ DIFFICULTY ○ ○ ○ ○ ○ RATING ☆ ☆ ☆ ☆ ☆

INGREDIENTS

DIRECTIONS

GLASS

GARNISH

NOTES

COCKTAIL ....

📅 DATE .... DIFFICULTY ○ ○ ○ ○ ○ RATING ☆ ☆ ☆ ☆ ☆

INGREDIENTS

....
....
....
....
....
....
....
....
....
....
....
....

DIRECTIONS

....
....
....
....
....
....
....
....
....
....
....
....
....

🍷 GLASS

🌿 GARNISH ....
....
....

📝 NOTES ....
....
....
....

COCKTAIL

01 DATE _____   **DIFFICULTY** ○ ○ ○ ○ ○   **RATING** ☆ ☆ ☆ ☆ ☆

INGREDIENTS

DIRECTIONS

GLASS

GARNISH _____

NOTES _____

COCKTAIL

DATE _____   DIFFICULTY ○○○○○   RATING ☆☆☆☆☆

INGREDIENTS

DIRECTIONS

GLASS

GARNISH

NOTES

COCKTAIL

01 DATE .... DIFFICULTY ○ ○ ○ ○ ○ RATING ☆ ☆ ☆ ☆ ☆

INGREDIENTS

DIRECTIONS

GLASS

GARNISH

NOTES

COCKTAIL ....

📅 DATE ....   DIFFICULTY ⭘⭘⭘⭘⭘   RATING ☆☆☆☆☆

INGREDIENTS

DIRECTIONS

🍷 GLASS

💐 GARNISH ....

📝 NOTES ....

COCKTAIL

DATE .... **DIFFICULTY** ○ ○ ○ ○ ○ **RATING** ☆ ☆ ☆ ☆ ☆

INGREDIENTS

DIRECTIONS

GLASS

GARNISH

NOTES

34

COCKTAIL

DATE .... **DIFFICULTY** ○ ○ ○ ○ ○ **RATING** ☆ ☆ ☆ ☆ ☆

INGREDIENTS

DIRECTIONS

GLASS

GARNISH

NOTES

COCKTAIL

01 DATE .... DIFFICULTY ○ ○ ○ ○ ○   RATING ☆ ☆ ☆ ☆ ☆

INGREDIENTS

....
....
....
....
....
....
....
....
....
....
....
....

DIRECTIONS

....
....
....
....
....
....
....
....
....
....
....
....

GLASS

GARNISH ....
....
....

NOTES ....
....
....
....

COCKTAIL ....

📅 DATE ....   DIFFICULTY ○○○○○   RATING ☆☆☆☆☆

🍾 INGREDIENTS

🍸 DIRECTIONS

🥂 GLASS

🌿 GARNISH ....
....
....

📝 NOTES ....
....
....
....

COCKTAIL

01 DATE .... DIFFICULTY ○○○○○ RATING ☆☆☆☆☆

INGREDIENTS

DIRECTIONS

GLASS

GARNISH

NOTES

COCKTAIL

📅 DATE _____   DIFFICULTY ○ ○ ○ ○ ○   RATING ☆ ☆ ☆ ☆ ☆

INGREDIENTS

DIRECTIONS

🍷 GLASS

🌿 GARNISH

📝 NOTES

COCKTAIL

DATE .... DIFFICULTY ○ ○ ○ ○ ○ RATING ☆ ☆ ☆ ☆ ☆

INGREDIENTS

DIRECTIONS

GLASS

GARNISH

NOTES

COCKTAIL ....

01 DATE .... DIFFICULTY ○○○○○ RATING ☆☆☆☆☆

INGREDIENTS

DIRECTIONS

GLASS

GARNISH ....
....
....

NOTES ....
....
....
....

COCKTAIL

DATE .... DIFFICULTY ○ ○ ○ ○ ○ RATING ☆ ☆ ☆ ☆ ☆

INGREDIENTS

DIRECTIONS

GLASS

GARNISH

NOTES

COCKTAIL ....

DATE .... **DIFFICULTY** ○ ○ ○ ○ ○ **RATING** ☆ ☆ ☆ ☆ ☆

INGREDIENTS

DIRECTIONS

GLASS

GARNISH ....

NOTES ....

COCKTAIL ....

📅 DATE .... DIFFICULTY ○ ○ ○ ○ ○ RATING ☆ ☆ ☆ ☆ ☆

INGREDIENTS

DIRECTIONS

🍷 GLASS

🍹 GARNISH ....

📝 NOTES ....

COCKTAIL ....

📅 DATE ....   DIFFICULTY ○○○○○   RATING ☆☆☆☆☆

🍾 INGREDIENTS

🍸 DIRECTIONS

🍷 GLASS

🌿 GARNISH ....

📝 NOTES ....

COCKTAIL _____

INGREDIENTS

DIRECTIONS

🍷 GLASS

🌿 GARNISH _____

📝 NOTES _____

COCKTAIL ....

INGREDIENTS

DIRECTIONS

🍷 GLASS

🌿 GARNISH ....
....
....

📝 NOTES ....
....
....
....

COCKTAIL

01 DATE _____ DIFFICULTY ○○○○○ RATING ☆☆☆☆☆

INGREDIENTS

DIRECTIONS

GLASS

GARNISH

NOTES

COCKTAIL ....

📅 DATE .... DIFFICULTY ○○○○○ RATING ☆☆☆☆☆

INGREDIENTS

....
....
....
....
....
....
....
....
....
....
....
....

DIRECTIONS

....
....
....
....
....
....
....
....
....
....
....
....
....

GLASS

GARNISH ....
....
....
....

NOTES ....
....
....
....
....

COCKTAIL

01 DATE .... DIFFICULTY ○ ○ ○ ○ ○   RATING ☆ ☆ ☆ ☆ ☆

INGREDIENTS

DIRECTIONS

GLASS

GARNISH

NOTES

COCKTAIL

DATE .... DIFFICULTY ○ ○ ○ ○ ○ RATING ☆ ☆ ☆ ☆ ☆

INGREDIENTS

DIRECTIONS

GLASS

GARNISH

NOTES

COCKTAIL _____

📅 DATE _____   DIFFICULTY ○ ○ ○ ○ ○   RATING ☆ ☆ ☆ ☆ ☆

INGREDIENTS

DIRECTIONS

🍷 GLASS

💐 GARNISH _____

📝 NOTES _____

COCKTAIL ....

📅 DATE ....   DIFFICULTY ○○○○○   RATING ☆☆☆☆☆

🍾 INGREDIENTS

....
....
....
....
....
....
....
....
....
....
....
....

🍸 DIRECTIONS

....
....
....
....
....
....
....
....
....
....
....
....
....
....

🍷 GLASS

🌿 GARNISH ....
....
....
....

📝 NOTES ....
....
....
....
....

COCKTAIL ....

📅 DATE .... DIFFICULTY ○○○○○ RATING ☆☆☆☆☆

🍾 INGREDIENTS

🍸 DIRECTIONS

🍷 GLASS

💐 GARNISH ....

📝 NOTES ....

COCKTAIL _____

📅 DATE _____ DIFFICULTY ○ ○ ○ ○ ○   RATING ☆ ☆ ☆ ☆ ☆

INGREDIENTS

_____ _____
_____ _____
_____ _____
_____ _____
_____ _____
_____ _____
_____ _____
_____ _____
_____ _____
_____ _____

DIRECTIONS

_____
_____
_____
_____
_____
_____
_____
_____
_____
_____
_____
_____

GLASS

GARNISH _____
_____
_____

NOTES _____
_____
_____
_____

COCKTAIL _____

📅 DATE _____ DIFFICULTY ○ ○ ○ ○ ○   RATING ☆ ☆ ☆ ☆ ☆

INGREDIENTS

DIRECTIONS

🍷 GLASS

💐 GARNISH

📝 NOTES

COCKTAIL

01 DATE _____   DIFFICULTY ○ ○ ○ ○ ○   RATING ☆ ☆ ☆ ☆ ☆

INGREDIENTS

DIRECTIONS

GLASS

GARNISH

NOTES

COCKTAIL

DATE _____ **DIFFICULTY** ○ ○ ○ ○ ○   **RATING** ☆ ☆ ☆ ☆ ☆

INGREDIENTS

DIRECTIONS

GLASS

GARNISH

NOTES

COCKTAIL ....

DATE .... DIFFICULTY ○ ○ ○ ○ ○ RATING ☆ ☆ ☆ ☆ ☆

INGREDIENTS

DIRECTIONS

GLASS

GARNISH ....

NOTES ....

COCKTAIL

📅 DATE _____   DIFFICULTY ○○○○○   RATING ☆☆☆☆☆

🍾 INGREDIENTS

🍸 DIRECTIONS

🍷 GLASS

🌿 GARNISH

📝 NOTES

COCKTAIL ....

01 DATE ....   DIFFICULTY ○○○○○   RATING ☆☆☆☆☆

INGREDIENTS

DIRECTIONS

GLASS

GARNISH ....

NOTES ....

COCKTAIL

01 DATE .... **DIFFICULTY** ○ ○ ○ ○ ○ **RATING** ☆ ☆ ☆ ☆ ☆

INGREDIENTS

DIRECTIONS

GLASS

GARNISH

NOTES

COCKTAIL

01 DATE ....   **DIFFICULTY** ○ ○ ○ ○ ○   **RATING** ☆ ☆ ☆ ☆ ☆

INGREDIENTS

DIRECTIONS

GLASS

GARNISH

NOTES

COCKTAIL

DATE .... DIFFICULTY ○ ○ ○ ○ ○　　　RATING ☆ ☆ ☆ ☆ ☆

INGREDIENTS

DIRECTIONS

GLASS

GARNISH

NOTES

COCKTAIL ....

📅 DATE ....   DIFFICULTY ○○○○○   RATING ☆☆☆☆☆

INGREDIENTS

_____
_____
_____
_____
_____
_____
_____
_____
_____
_____
_____

DIRECTIONS

_____
_____
_____
_____
_____
_____
_____
_____
_____
_____
_____
_____

GLASS

GARNISH _____
_____
_____

NOTES _____
_____
_____

COCKTAIL

DATE .... **DIFFICULTY** ○ ○ ○ ○ ○   **RATING** ☆ ☆ ☆ ☆ ☆

INGREDIENTS

DIRECTIONS

GLASS

GARNISH

NOTES

COCKTAIL

DATE .... **DIFFICULTY** ○ ○ ○ ○ ○   **RATING** ☆ ☆ ☆ ☆ ☆

INGREDIENTS

DIRECTIONS

GLASS

GARNISH

NOTES

COCKTAIL

01 DATE _____ **DIFFICULTY** ○ ○ ○ ○ ○ **RATING** ☆ ☆ ☆ ☆ ☆

INGREDIENTS

DIRECTIONS

GLASS

GARNISH

NOTES

COCKTAIL ....

📅 DATE .... DIFFICULTY ○○○○○ RATING ☆☆☆☆☆

🍾 INGREDIENTS

🍸 DIRECTIONS

🍷 GLASS

💐 GARNISH ....

📝 NOTES ....

COCKTAIL

01 DATE _____   DIFFICULTY ○ ○ ○ ○ ○   RATING ☆ ☆ ☆ ☆ ☆

INGREDIENTS

DIRECTIONS

GLASS

GARNISH

NOTES

COCKTAIL

DATE .... DIFFICULTY ○ ○ ○ ○ ○ RATING ☆ ☆ ☆ ☆ ☆

INGREDIENTS

DIRECTIONS

GLASS

GARNISH

NOTES

COCKTAIL

01 DATE .... DIFFICULTY ○ ○ ○ ○ ○   RATING ☆ ☆ ☆ ☆ ☆

INGREDIENTS

....
....
....
....
....
....
....
....
....
....
....

DIRECTIONS

....
....
....
....
....
....
....
....
....
....
....

GLASS

GARNISH ....
....
....
....

NOTES ....
....
....
....
....

COCKTAIL

DATE .... DIFFICULTY ○○○○○ RATING ☆☆☆☆☆

INGREDIENTS

DIRECTIONS

GLASS

GARNISH

NOTES

COCKTAIL

DATE .... DIFFICULTY ○○○○○ RATING ☆☆☆☆☆

INGREDIENTS

DIRECTIONS

GLASS

GARNISH

NOTES

COCKTAIL

📅 DATE .... DIFFICULTY ○○○○○ RATING ☆☆☆☆☆

🍾 INGREDIENTS

🍸 DIRECTIONS

🍷 GLASS

🌿 GARNISH

📝 NOTES

COCKTAIL

01 DATE .... DIFFICULTY ○○○○○ RATING ☆☆☆☆☆

INGREDIENTS

DIRECTIONS

GLASS

GARNISH

NOTES

COCKTAIL

DATE .... **DIFFICULTY** ○○○○○ **RATING** ☆☆☆☆☆

INGREDIENTS

DIRECTIONS

GLASS

GARNISH

NOTES

COCKTAIL

DATE _____   DIFFICULTY ○ ○ ○ ○ ○   RATING ☆ ☆ ☆ ☆ ☆

INGREDIENTS

DIRECTIONS

GLASS

GARNISH

NOTES

COCKTAIL

01 DATE .... DIFFICULTY ○○○○○ RATING ☆☆☆☆☆

INGREDIENTS

DIRECTIONS

GLASS

GARNISH

NOTES

COCKTAIL ....

📅 DATE .... DIFFICULTY ○ ○ ○ ○ ○ RATING ☆ ☆ ☆ ☆ ☆

🍾 INGREDIENTS

🍸 DIRECTIONS

🍷 GLASS

💐 GARNISH

📝 NOTES

COCKTAIL _____

DATE _____   DIFFICULTY ○ ○ ○ ○ ○   RATING ☆ ☆ ☆ ☆ ☆

INGREDIENTS

DIRECTIONS

GLASS

GARNISH

NOTES

COCKTAIL

01 DATE _____   DIFFICULTY ○ ○ ○ ○ ○   RATING ☆ ☆ ☆ ☆ ☆

INGREDIENTS

DIRECTIONS

GLASS

GARNISH

NOTES

COCKTAIL

01 DATE .... DIFFICULTY ○ ○ ○ ○ ○   RATING ☆ ☆ ☆ ☆ ☆

INGREDIENTS

DIRECTIONS

GLASS

GARNISH

NOTES

COCKTAIL

01 DATE .... DIFFICULTY ○ ○ ○ ○ ○   RATING ☆ ☆ ☆ ☆ ☆

INGREDIENTS

DIRECTIONS

GLASS

GARNISH

NOTES

COCKTAIL ....

📅 DATE .... **DIFFICULTY** ○○○○○ **RATING** ☆☆☆☆☆

🍾 INGREDIENTS

🍸 DIRECTIONS

🍷 GLASS

🌿 GARNISH ....

📝 NOTES ....

COCKTAIL

01 DATE .... **DIFFICULTY** ○ ○ ○ ○ ○ **RATING** ☆ ☆ ☆ ☆ ☆

INGREDIENTS

DIRECTIONS

GLASS

GARNISH

NOTES

COCKTAIL

DATE .... DIFFICULTY ○ ○ ○ ○ ○ RATING ☆ ☆ ☆ ☆ ☆

INGREDIENTS

DIRECTIONS

GLASS

GARNISH

NOTES

COCKTAIL

DATE .... DIFFICULTY ○ ○ ○ ○ ○   RATING ☆ ☆ ☆ ☆ ☆

INGREDIENTS

DIRECTIONS

GLASS

GARNISH

NOTES

COCKTAIL

📅 DATE .... DIFFICULTY ⭕⭕⭕⭕⭕ RATING ☆☆☆☆☆

INGREDIENTS

DIRECTIONS

🍷 GLASS

💐 GARNISH

📝 NOTES

COCKTAIL

DATE _____ DIFFICULTY ○ ○ ○ ○ ○ RATING ☆ ☆ ☆ ☆ ☆

INGREDIENTS

DIRECTIONS

GLASS

GARNISH

NOTES

COCKTAIL

DATE .... **DIFFICULTY** ○○○○○ **RATING** ☆☆☆☆☆

INGREDIENTS

DIRECTIONS

GLASS

GARNISH

NOTES

COCKTAIL

01 DATE .... DIFFICULTY ○○○○○ RATING ☆☆☆☆☆

INGREDIENTS

DIRECTIONS

GLASS

GARNISH

NOTES

COCKTAIL

DATE _____ DIFFICULTY ○○○○○ RATING ☆☆☆☆☆

INGREDIENTS

DIRECTIONS

GLASS

GARNISH

NOTES

COCKTAIL

01 DATE ....   DIFFICULTY ○ ○ ○ ○ ○   RATING ☆ ☆ ☆ ☆ ☆

INGREDIENTS

DIRECTIONS

🍷 GLASS

💐 GARNISH

📝 NOTES

COCKTAIL

DATE

DIFFICULTY ○ ○ ○ ○ ○

RATING ☆ ☆ ☆ ☆ ☆

INGREDIENTS

DIRECTIONS

GLASS

GARNISH

NOTES

COCKTAIL

DATE _____   DIFFICULTY ○ ○ ○ ○ ○   RATING ☆ ☆ ☆ ☆ ☆

INGREDIENTS

DIRECTIONS

GLASS

GARNISH

NOTES

COCKTAIL ....

📅 DATE ....   DIFFICULTY ○○○○○   RATING ☆☆☆☆☆

🍾 INGREDIENTS

....
....
....
....
....
....
....
....
....
....
....
....

🍸 DIRECTIONS

....
....
....
....
....
....
....
....
....
....
....
....
....

🍷 GLASS

🌿 GARNISH ....
....
....
....

📝 NOTES ....
....
....
....
....

COCKTAIL

DATE .... **DIFFICULTY** ○ ○ ○ ○ ○   **RATING** ☆ ☆ ☆ ☆ ☆

INGREDIENTS

DIRECTIONS

GLASS

GARNISH

NOTES

COCKTAIL

DATE .... **DIFFICULTY** ○○○○○ **RATING** ☆☆☆☆☆

INGREDIENTS

DIRECTIONS

GLASS

GARNISH

NOTES

COCKTAIL

DATE ....

DIFFICULTY ○ ○ ○ ○ ○

RATING ☆ ☆ ☆ ☆ ☆

INGREDIENTS

DIRECTIONS

GLASS

GARNISH

NOTES

COCKTAIL

DATE .... DIFFICULTY ○○○○○ RATING ☆☆☆☆☆

INGREDIENTS

DIRECTIONS

GLASS

GARNISH

NOTES

COCKTAIL

01 DATE .... DIFFICULTY ○ ○ ○ ○ ○ RATING ☆ ☆ ☆ ☆ ☆

INGREDIENTS

DIRECTIONS

GLASS

GARNISH

NOTES

COCKTAIL ....

📅 DATE .... DIFFICULTY ○ ○ ○ ○ ○ RATING ☆ ☆ ☆ ☆ ☆

INGREDIENTS

....
....
....
....
....
....
....
....
....
....
....
....
....

DIRECTIONS

....
....
....
....
....
....
....
....
....
....
....
....

🍷 GLASS

🌿 GARNISH ....
....
....

📝 NOTES ....
....
....
....

COCKTAIL _____

📅 DATE _____   DIFFICULTY ○○○○○   RATING ☆☆☆☆☆

🍾 INGREDIENTS

🍸 DIRECTIONS

🍷 GLASS

💐 GARNISH _____

📝 NOTES _____

COCKTAIL ....

01 DATE .... DIFFICULTY ○○○○○ RATING ☆☆☆☆☆

INGREDIENTS

DIRECTIONS

....
....
....
....
....
....
....
....
....
....
....
....

GLASS

GARNISH ....
....
....
....

NOTES ....
....
....
....
....

COCKTAIL

DATE .... **DIFFICULTY** ○ ○ ○ ○ ○ **RATING** ☆ ☆ ☆ ☆ ☆

INGREDIENTS

DIRECTIONS

GLASS

GARNISH

NOTES

COCKTAIL

DATE

DIFFICULTY ○ ○ ○ ○ ○

RATING ☆ ☆ ☆ ☆ ☆

INGREDIENTS

DIRECTIONS

GLASS

GARNISH

NOTES

COCKTAIL

DATE ....   DIFFICULTY ○○○○○   RATING ☆☆☆☆☆

INGREDIENTS

....
....
....
....
....
....
....
....
....
....
....

DIRECTIONS

....
....
....
....
....
....
....
....
....
....
....

GLASS

GARNISH ....
....
....

NOTES ....
....
....
....

COCKTAIL ....

📅 DATE ....   DIFFICULTY ○ ○ ○ ○ ○   RATING ☆ ☆ ☆ ☆ ☆

🍾 INGREDIENTS

🍸 DIRECTIONS

🍷 GLASS

🌿 GARNISH ....
....
....
....

📓 NOTES ....
....
....
....
....

COCKTAIL

DATE .... **DIFFICULTY** ○ ○ ○ ○ ○ **RATING** ☆ ☆ ☆ ☆ ☆

INGREDIENTS

DIRECTIONS

GLASS

GARNISH

NOTES

COCKTAIL

01 DATE .... **DIFFICULTY** ○○○○○ **RATING** ☆☆☆☆☆

INGREDIENTS

DIRECTIONS

GLASS

GARNISH

NOTES

COCKTAIL ....

📅 DATE .... DIFFICULTY ○ ○ ○ ○ ○   RATING ☆ ☆ ☆ ☆ ☆

INGREDIENTS

DIRECTIONS

🍷 GLASS

💐 GARNISH ....

📝 NOTES ....

COCKTAIL

INGREDIENTS

DIRECTIONS

GLASS

GARNISH

NOTES

COCKTAIL

01 DATE _____   **DIFFICULTY** ○ ○ ○ ○ ○   **RATING** ☆ ☆ ☆ ☆ ☆

INGREDIENTS

DIRECTIONS

GLASS

GARNISH

NOTES

COCKTAIL

01 DATE .... DIFFICULTY ○○○○○ RATING ☆☆☆☆☆

INGREDIENTS

DIRECTIONS

GLASS

GARNISH

NOTES

COCKTAIL

📅 DATE _____   DIFFICULTY ○ ○ ○ ○ ○   RATING ☆ ☆ ☆ ☆ ☆

INGREDIENTS

DIRECTIONS

🍷 GLASS

💐 GARNISH

📝 NOTES

COCKTAIL

📅 **DATE** _____ **DIFFICULTY** ○ ○ ○ ○ ○ **RATING** ☆ ☆ ☆ ☆ ☆

INGREDIENTS

DIRECTIONS

🍷 **GLASS**

🌿 **GARNISH**

📝 **NOTES**

COCKTAIL

DATE .... **DIFFICULTY** ○ ○ ○ ○ ○ **RATING** ☆ ☆ ☆ ☆ ☆

INGREDIENTS

DIRECTIONS

GLASS

GARNISH

NOTES

COCKTAIL

DATE ....

DIFFICULTY ○ ○ ○ ○ ○

RATING ☆ ☆ ☆ ☆ ☆

INGREDIENTS

DIRECTIONS

GLASS

GARNISH

NOTES

Contact:

Gerald Curk Marketing & Design
Waldschmidtstraße 9 • 93051 Regensburg
GERMANY

Any questions or suggestions: servus@curk.de

All rights reserved.

Made in United States
North Haven, CT
29 January 2024

48044979R00075